IMAGINE. CREATE. REPEAT.

COPYRIGHT & PERMISSIONS

Please feel free to take photos of this notebook (or your use of it) for the purpose of social media sharing. Please do not photograph the entire notebook.

Pencil Icon made by Pixel perfect from www.flaticon.com
Research Icon made by Freepik from www.flaticon.com
Brainstorming Icon made by Eucalyp from www.flaticon.com

Table of Contents

Brainstorm — 5

Story Development — 7

Plot Summary — 13

What Could Happen — 15

Story Structure — 16

Plot Points — 19

Story Board — 24

Characters — 27

Setting — 38

Chapters & Scenes — 54

Research — 95

Notes — 99

HOW TO USE

Plotting a novel can be fun and also overwhelming. The aim of the StoryNote is to be a centralized space for all things related to your story.

Use the Brainstorming pages to write any and every idea.

Use the Story Development question to wrangle in your ideas and develop a plot for your story.

Fill in the Plot Summary page once you've gotten a grasp on where you'd like your story to go.

Use the Plot Point pages to fill in the rest of the story. The squares next to the plot points can be used to order your plot points so you don't have to worry about writing the events down in chronological order.

Use the Story Board to order the plot points into chapters. * Tip: Use sticky notes to easily reorder the chapters

The different types of Character pages are ideal for main characters, secondary characters, and tertiary characters.

Use the Setting pages to remember important details about major and frequently used settings.

Finally, use the Chapter pages to summarize chapters and break the events down in scene.

Happy Writing !

BRAINSTORM

a conference technique of solving specific problems, amassing information, stimulating creative thinking, developing new ideas

BRAINSTORM

a conference technique of solving specific problems, amassing information, stimulating creative thinking, developing new ideas

STORY DEVELOPMENT

the act, process, or result of developing a story

Story Idea

....
....
....
....
....
....
....

What story do you want to tell? Why?

....
....
....
....
....
....
....

What happens to trigger the story?

....
....
....
....
....
....

Who is the main character? What are they like?

....
....
....
....
....
....

What internal and external conflicts does the main character face at the beginning of the story?

Where does the main character stand on these conflicts at the end of the story?

What is the main character's goal at the beginning of the story? Does this goal change during the story?

Who or what is the antagonist or opposing force?

What is the antagonist's goal? What drives them towards this goal?

How does the antagonist plan on achieving their goal?

Are the protagonist and the antagonist similar? How so?

What is the relationship or connection between the protagonist and the antagonist?

Where does the story take place? (Time period, country, city, another dimension)

Does anything make this world unique? If so, what?

What type of government exists?

What type of people or creatures exist in this world?

What type of clothing do they wear? Does the main character's clothing set them apart from others?

What is the culture like? Languages? Food? Traditions?

What type of technology exists? How advanced is it?

What type of transportation is used?

NOTES

a brief record of something written down to assist the memory or for future reference

PLOT SUMMARY

a connected sequence of events that make up a story

What is the main story?

What is the subplot?

What is the story's theme?

PLOT SUMMARY

a connected sequence of events that make up a story

Summarize the plot.

Whose perspective is the story told from? First, Second, or Third point of view? Why this point of view?

What do you want to achieve by writing this story?

WHAT COULD HAPPEN ?

let your imagination run wild

Possible Beginnings

-
-
-
-
-
-
-
-
-
-

Possible Endings

-
-
-
-
-
-
-
-
-
-

Plot Twists

-
-
-
-
-

STORY STRUCTURE

the structural framework of the story's key conflicts, main characters, setting and events

Act One
Setup

Beginning ——————

Inciting Incident ——————

Plot Point # 1 ——————

Act Two
Confrontation

Fun & Games ——————

Pinch Point # 1 ——————

Midpoint ——————

Pinch Point # 2 ——————

Black Moment ——————

Plot Point # 2 ——————

Act Three
Resolution

Climax ——————

Denouement ——————

Final Image ——————

Summary

STORY STRUCTURE

the structural framework of the story's key conflicts, main characters, setting and events

Beginning (Hook)

Inciting Incident

Rising Action

Conflict

Climax

Falling Action

Ending

Resolution

NOTES

a brief record of something written down to assist the memory or for future reference

PLOT POINTS

a significant event within a plot which turns the action in another direction

PLOT POINTS

a significant event within a plot which turns the action in another direction

NOTES

a brief record of something written down to assist the memory or for future reference

a structure technique which captures a scene or plot point in a visual aspect or brief summary

STORY BOARD

a structure technique which captures a scene or plot point in a visual aspect or brief summary

CREATING AWESOME CHARACTERS

characterization: the creation or construction of a fictional character

What are the character's needs and wants? What are their goals? Are their wants and/or goals what they really need to achieve or simple what the character thinks they need to achieve?

Why do they want to accomplish this goal? How will it improve their life? Or will accomplishing this goal actually destroy their life?

Does this character have any quirks?

What flaws does this character have? How do these flaws impact their life and the choices they make?

Does this character have family and friends? How do these people influence their life?

How does the character perceive themselves? Does this differ from how others may perceive them?

How does the character interact with others? Are they rude? Do they speak abruptly? Are they shy?

What are their habits and routines? How did these habits/routines come about?

What makes them angry? Why?

Do they have triggers? What happened to develop those triggers?

What does happiness mean to the character? What makes them happy? How do they express happiness?

What traits may the antagonist have that makes them human/believable?

Are the protagonist and the antagonist similar in anyway? Do they share a common goal? How do their tactics for achieving this goal differ?

How does the character process negative emotions?

How do past experiences affect how they make decisions?

Cast of Characters

Name	Role	Description

PROTAGONIST

Name:

....

Physical Traits:

....

....

....

Unique Features/ Abilities:

....

Personality:

....

....

....

Mannerisms & Habits:

....

....

....

Triggers:

....

....

....

Backstory:

....

....

....

....

....

Goals & Motivation:

....

....

Notes:

....

....

ANTAGONIST

Name:

Physical Traits:

Unique Features/ Abilities:

Personality:

Mannerisms & Habits:

Triggers:

Backstory:

Goals & Motivation:

Notes:

CHARACTER

Name:

Physical Traits:

Unique Features/ Abilities:

Personality:

Mannerisms & Habits:

Triggers:

Backstory:

Goals & Motivation:

Notes:

CHARACTER

Name:

....

Physical Traits:

....

....

....

....

Unique Features/ Abilities:

....

Personality:

....

....

....

Mannerisms & Habits:

....

....

....

Triggers:

....

....

....

Backstory:

....

....

....

....

....

....

Goals & Motivation:

....

....

Notes:

....

....

....

CHARACTER

Name:

Physical Traits:

Unique Features/ Abilities:

Personality:

Mannerisms & Habits:

Triggers:

Backstory:

Goals & Motivation:

Notes:

CHARACTER

Name:

....

Physical Traits:

....

....

....

....

Unique Features/ Abilities:

....

Personality:

....

....

Mannerisms & Habits:

....

....

....

Triggers:

....

....

....

Backstory:

....

....

....

....

....

....

Goals & Motivation:

....

....

Notes:

....

....

....

CHARACTER

Name:

Physical Traits:

Unique Features/ Abilities:

Personality:

Mannerisms & Habits:

Triggers:

Backstory:

Goals & Motivation:

Notes:

CHARACTER

Name:

Name:

Name:

Name:

Name:

CHARACTER

Name:

Name:

Name:

Name:

Name:

NOTES

a brief record of something written down to assist the memory or for future reference

SETTING

the place or type of surroundings where something is positioned or where an event takes place

Name

....

Place   Time Period

....

Season: Spring   Summer   Autumn   Winter

Description:

....

....

....

....

....

Protagonist POV:

....

....

Antagonist POV:

....

....

What makes this setting unique?

....

....

What are some common sounds heard here?

....

What does it smell like?

....

Does this place bring back memories for the characters? Will the characters create memories here?

....

....

How does the setting make the characters feel? Emotionally? Physically? Why?

....

....

SETTING

the place or type of surroundings where something is positioned or where an event takes place

Name

Place   Time Period

Season: Spring   Summer   Autumn   Winter

Description:

Protagonist POV:

Antagonist POV:

What makes this setting unique?

What are some common sounds heard here?

What does it smell like?

Does this place bring back memories for the characters? Will the characters create memories here?

How does the setting make the characters feel? Emotionally? Physically? Why?

SETTING

---

the place or type of surroundings where something is positioned or where an event takes place

Name

Place　　　　　　　　　　　　　　　　　　　　　　　　Time Period

Season:　　　　　Spring　　　Summer　　　Autumn　　　Winter

Description:

Protagonist POV:

Antagonist POV:

What makes this setting unique?

What are some common sounds heard here?

What does it smell like?

Does this place bring back memories for the characters? Will the characters create memories here?

How does the setting make the characters feel? Emotionally? Physically? Why?

SETTING

the place or type of surroundings where something is positioned or where an event takes place

Name

....

Place

Time Period

....

Season: Spring   Summer   Autumn   Winter

Description:

....

....

....

....

....

Protagonist POV:

....

....

Antagonist POV:

....

....

What makes this setting unique?

....

....

What are some common sounds heard here?

....

What does it smell like?

....

....

Does this place bring back memories for the characters? Will the characters create memories here?

....

....

How does the setting make the characters feel? Emotionally? Physically? Why?

....

....

....

SETTING

the place or type of surroundings where something is positioned or where an event takes place

Name

....

Place   Time Period

....

Season: Spring   Summer   Autumn   Winter

Description:

....

....

....

....

....

Protagonist POV:

....

....

Antagonist POV:

....

....

What makes this setting unique?

....

....

What are some common sounds heard here?

....

What does it smell like?

....

Does this place bring back memories for the characters? Will the characters create memories here?

....

....

How does the setting make the characters feel? Emotionally? Physically? Why?

....

....

SETTING

---

the place or type of surroundings where something is positioned or where an event takes place

Name

....

Place   Time Period

....

Season: Spring   Summer   Autumn   Winter

Description:

....

....

....

....

....

Protagonist POV:

....

....

Antagonist POV:

....

....

What makes this setting unique?

....

....

What are some common sounds heard here?

....

What does it smell like?

....

Does this place bring back memories for the characters? Will the characters create memories here?

....

....

How does the setting make the characters feel? Emotionally? Physically? Why?

....

....

SETTING

Name

....

Place   Time Period

....

Season: Spring   Summer   Autumn   Winter

Description:

....

....

....

....

....

Protagonist POV:

....

....

Antagonist POV:

....

....

What makes this setting unique?

....

....

What are some common sounds heard here?

....

What does it smell like?

....

....

Does this place bring back memories for the characters? Will the characters create memories here?

....

....

How does the setting make the characters feel? Emotionally? Physically? Why?

....

....

SETTING

the place or type of surroundings where something is positioned or where an event takes place

Name

....

Place   Time Period

....

Season: Spring   Summer   Autumn   Winter

Description:

....

....

....

....

....

Protagonist POV:

....

....

Antagonist POV:

....

....

What makes this setting unique?

....

....

What are some common sounds heard here?

....

What does it smell like?

....

Does this place bring back memories for the characters? Will the characters create memories here?

....

....

How does the setting make the characters feel? Emotionally? Physically? Why?

....

....

SETTING

the place or type of surroundings where something is positioned or where an event takes place

Name

....

Place   Time Period

....

Season: Spring   Summer   Autumn   Winter

Description:

Protagonist POV:

Antagonist POV:

What makes this setting unique?

What are some common sounds heard here?

What does it smell like?

Does this place bring back memories for the characters? Will the characters create memories here?

How does the setting make the characters feel? Emotionally? Physically? Why?

SETTING

the place or type of surroundings where something is positioned or where an event takes place

Name

Place   Time Period

Season: Spring   Summer   Autumn   Winter

Description:

Protagonist POV:

Antagonist POV:

What makes this setting unique?

What are some common sounds heard here?

What does it smell like?

Does this place bring back memories for the characters? Will the characters create memories here?

How does the setting make the characters feel? Emotionally? Physically? Why?

SETTING

the place or type of surroundings where something is positioned or where an event takes place

Name

....

Place   Time Period

....

Season: Spring   Summer   Autumn   Winter

Description:

....

....

....

....

....

Protagonist POV:

....

....

Antagonist POV:

....

....

What makes this setting unique?

....

....

What are some common sounds heard here?

....

What does it smell like?

....

Does this place bring back memories for the characters? Will the characters create memories here?

....

....

How does the setting make the characters feel? Emotionally? Physically? Why?

....

....

....

SETTING

the place or type of surroundings where something is positioned or where an event takes place

Name

....

Place   Time Period

Season: Spring   Summer   Autumn   Winter

Description:

Protagonist POV:

Antagonist POV:

What makes this setting unique?

What are some common sounds heard here?

What does it smell like?

Does this place bring back memories for the characters? Will the characters create memories here?

How does the setting make the characters feel? Emotionally? Physically? Why?

NOTES

a brief record of something written down to assist the memory or for future reference

NOTES

a brief record of something written down to assist the memory or for future reference

NOTES

a brief record of something written down to assist the memory or for future reference

CREATING CHAPTERS & SCENES

How does this scene advance the story? Does it develop the plot? What needs to happen to advance the story?

What is the pacing of the scene ?

How does this chapter or scene work with the other chapters and scenes?

Who is in the scene?

Is each character in the scene necessary? What is their purpose?

What conflict takes place in this scene? Is there any tension or suspense?

What is at stake?

What's the setting like? What are the characters' perspective of the setting? Do they all share the same perspec-

Does the setting impact the story? How so?

What are the character's immediate goals? What opposition do they face?

How do the character or characters feel mentally/physically?

How do the characters feel towards each other?

Are the characters' actions or reactions believable?

How do the characters feel at the beginning of the scene vs. the end of the scene?

What should the outcome of the scene be? How does the story change if the outcome is different?

CHAPTER

Summary

Scene 1

Setting:

Scene 2

Setting:

CHAPTER

Scene 3

Setting:

Scene 4

Setting:

Scene 5

Setting:

CHAPTER

Summary

Scene 1

Setting:

Scene 2

Setting:

CHAPTER

Scene 3

Setting:

Scene 4

Setting:

Scene 5

Setting:

CHAPTER

Summary

Scene 1

Setting:

Scene 2

Setting:

CHAPTER

Scene 3

Setting:

Scene 4

Setting:

Scene 5

Setting:

CHAPTER

Summary

....

....

....

....

....

....

....

....

....

Scene 1

Setting:

....

....

....

....

....

....

....

....

....

....

Scene 2

Setting:

....

....

....

....

....

....

....

CHAPTER

Scene 3

Setting:

Scene 4

Setting:

Scene 5

Setting:

CHAPTER

Summary

Scene 1

Setting:

Scene 2

Setting:

CHAPTER

Scene 3

Setting:

Scene 4

Setting:

Scene 5

Setting:

CHAPTER

Summary

....
....
....
....
....
....
....
....
....

Scene 1

Setting:
....
....
....
....
....
....
....
....

Scene 2

Setting:
....
....
....
....
....
....

CHAPTER

Scene 3

Setting:

Scene 4

Setting:

Scene 5

Setting:

CHAPTER

Summary

....
....
....
....
....
....
....
....
....
....

Scene 1

Setting: ....
....
....
....
....
....
....
....
....
....
....

Scene 2

Setting: ....
....
....
....
....
....
....
....

CHAPTER

Scene 3

Setting:

Scene 4

Setting:

Scene 5

Setting:

CHAPTER

Summary

....
....
....
....
....
....
....
....
....

Scene 1

Setting: ....
....
....
....
....
....
....
....
....

Scene 2

Setting: ....
....
....
....
....
....
....

CHAPTER

Scene 3

Setting:

Scene 4

Setting:

Scene 5

Setting:

CHAPTER

Summary

....
....
....
....
....
....
....
....
....

Scene 1

Setting: ....
....
....
....
....
....
....
....
....

Scene 2

Setting: ....
....
....
....
....
....
....
....

CHAPTER

Scene 3

Setting:

Scene 4

Setting:

Scene 5

Setting:

CHAPTER

Summary

....

....

....

....

....

....

....

....

Scene 1

Setting: ....

....

....

....

....

....

....

....

Scene 2

Setting: ....

....

....

....

....

....

....

CHAPTER

Scene 3

Setting:

Scene 4

Setting:

Scene 5

Setting:

CHAPTER

Summary

....
....
....
....
....
....
....
....
....

Scene 1

Setting: ....
....
....
....
....
....
....
....
....

Scene 2

Setting: ....
....
....
....
....
....
....

CHAPTER

Scene 3

Setting:

Scene 4

Setting:

Scene 5

Setting:

CHAPTER

Summary

Scene 1

Setting:

Scene 2

Setting:

CHAPTER

Scene 3

Setting:

Scene 4

Setting:

Scene 5

Setting:

CHAPTER

Summary

Scene 1

Setting:

Scene 2

Setting:

CHAPTER

Scene 3

Setting:

Scene 4

Setting:

Scene 5

Setting:

CHAPTER

Summary

....

....

....

....

....

....

....

....

....

Scene 1

Setting: ....

....

....

....

....

....

....

....

....

....

Scene 2

Setting: ....

....

....

....

....

....

....

....

Chapter

Scene 3

Setting:

Scene 4

Setting:

Scene 5

Setting:

CHAPTER

Summary

....

....

....

....

....

....

....

....

Scene 1

Setting: ....

....

....

....

....

....

....

....

....

Scene 2

Setting: ....

....

....

....

....

....

....

....

CHAPTER

Scene 3

Setting:

Scene 4

Setting:

Scene 5

Setting:

CHAPTER

Summary

....
....
....
....
....
....
....
....

Scene 1

Setting: ....
....
....
....
....
....
....
....

Scene 2

Setting: ....
....
....
....
....
....
....

CHAPTER

Scene 3

Setting:

Scene 4

Setting:

Scene 5

Setting:

CHAPTER

Summary

....
....
....
....
....
....
....
....

Scene 1

Setting:...
....
....
....
....
....
....
....
....
....

Scene 2

Setting:...
....
....
....
....
....
....

CHAPTER

Scene 3

Setting:

Scene 4

Setting:

Scene 5

Setting:

CHAPTER

Summary

Scene 1

Setting:

Scene 2

Setting:

CHAPTER

Scene 3

Setting:

Scene 4

Setting:

Scene 5

Setting:

CHAPTER

Summary

....
....
....
....
....
....
....
....
....

Scene 1

Setting:
....
....
....
....
....
....
....
....
....

Scene 2

Setting:
....
....
....
....
....
....
....

CHAPTER

Scene 3

Setting:

Scene 4

Setting:

Scene 5

Setting:

CHAPTER

Summary

....
....
....
....
....
....
....
....

Scene 1

Setting: ....
....
....
....
....
....
....
....

Scene 2

Setting: ....
....
....
....
....
....
....

CHAPTER

Scene 3

Setting:

Scene 4

Setting:

Scene 5

Setting:

NOTES

a brief record of something written down to assist the memory or for future reference

RESEARCH

diligent and systematic inquiry or investigation into a subject in order to discover or revise facts and theories

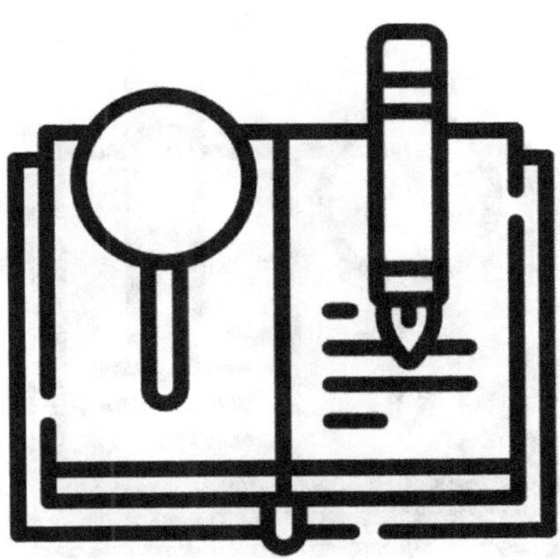

RESEARCH

diligent and systematic inquiry or investigation into a subject in order to discover or revise facts and theories

RESEARCH

diligent and systematic inquiry or investigation into a subject in order to discover or revise facts and theories

RESEARCH

diligent and systematic inquiry or investigation into a subject in order to discover or revise facts and theories

NOTES

a brief record of something written down to assist the memory or for future reference

NOTES

a brief record of something written down to assist the memory or for future reference

NOTES

a brief record of something written down to assist the memory or for future reference

NOTES

a brief record of something written down to assist the memory or for future reference

NOTES

a brief record of something written down to assist the memory or for future reference

THANK YOU

Hope you enjoyed using your workbook
Please let me know how you liked it and how it can improve

For other workbooks, worksheets & printables, please visit:

Etsy: StoryNote Worksheet
Instagram: storynoteco

Receive a free printable scene worsheet when you sign up at **StoryNoteCo.com** for new releases and updates !

Scene Worksheet

Chapter: _______________
Scene: _______________

Characters

____

____

____

____

____

Setting

Location: _______________________

Time of Day: _____________________

Season: __________________________

Weather: _________________________

Character Motivation

What do the character(s) want or need? How do they plan on achieving their goal? What are the consequences of their actions. How will the scene end?

____

____

____

____

____

Mood/Tone

What are the characters experiencing mentally or emotionally? Does the mood change throughout the scene? What causes the mood to change?

____

____

____

Scene Objective

What is the purpose of this scene? How does it advance the story? Does this scene work with othe scenes? What is the pacing of the scene?

____

____

____

____

____

Notes

____

____

____